The Wimp's Guide To

978 1 4451 1460 6 pb   978 1 4451 1464 4 eBook

978 1 4451 1461 3 pb   978 1 4451 1465 1 eBook

978 1 4451 1458 3 pb   978 1 4451 1462 0 eBook

978 1 4451 1459 0 pb   978 1 4451 1463 7 eBook

illustrated by
Dave Smith

KILLER
ANIMALS

by
Tracey Turner

LONDON·SYDNEY

First published in 2013
by Franklin Watts

Text © Tracey Turner 2013
Illustrations by Dave Smith
© Franklin Watts 2013
Cover design by Cathryn Gilbert
Layout by Jonathan Hair

Franklin Watts
338 Euston Road
London NW1 3BH

Franklin Watts Australia
Level 17/207 Kent Street
Sydney, NSW 2000

A CIP catalogue record for this book
is available from the British Library.

ISBN: 978 1 4451 1458 3

1   3   5   7   9   10   8   6   4   2

Printed in Great Britain

Franklin Watts is
a division of Hachette
Children's Books, an
Hachette UK company.

www.hachette.co.uk

CONTENTS

INTRODUCTION 6–9

DEADLY LAND PREDATORS 10–49

Polar Bears 12

Lions 20

Tigers 28

Snakes 36

Hippopotamuses 46

UNDERWATER KILLERS 50–69

Sharks 52

Box Jellyfish 60

Crocodiles 64

TINY ASSASSINS 70–87

Mosquitos 72

Spiders 76

Scorpions 84

LAST WORD 88–91

Your Wimp Rating 89

Glossary 92, Websites 93, Index 94

INTRODUCTION

There's nothing wrong with being a wimp. It makes perfect sense to be scared when, for example, **you spot a tiger in the undergrowth, or a scorpion in your shoe.**

There's a wimp inside all of us, and he or she is there for a very good reason — **to make us run away from killer wild animals very fast indeed.**

Animals that can kill are everywhere —
lurking on land, gliding through rivers and
seas, or crawling down your pants. They're
poised to scratch, sting, or tear off
your head. And
there's a surprisingly
wide variety. . .

⊙ VENOMOUS SNAKES
WITH A DEADLY BITE

⊙ FEROCIOUS BEARS
WITH MASSIVE JAWS

. . . then there's the . . .

CREEPY-CRAWLIES THAT CAN KILL WITH A SINGLE BITE

GIGANTIC FISH WITH 300 TEETH

. . . to name just a few. So, prepare yourself, because we're about to meet some of them. Actually, just in case, it might be wise not to set foot outside your front door until you have read this book. . .

In fact, to be on the safe side, you might want to look out for some protective clothing, insect repellent and perhaps a mosquito net.

So, now you're ready...

Come on!

Get a grip.

It's time to stare deadly beasts full in their snarling muzzles and snapping jaws. Read on to discover the horrifying details about killer animals and, most importantly, learn the best way to get away from them as fast as you possibly can . . . by harnessing the power of your inner wimp. **Gulp!**

Polar Bears

Actually, most deadly land predators aren't out to get you at all. They prey on different animals. Humans usually have to do something daft to get munched. **Phew!** What a relief. Hang on, though, because one or two predators definitely are out to get you, and one of them is the polar bear.

Aaarrggh!

WHAT COLOUR IS A
POLAR BEAR'S SKIN?
A) WHITE
B) YELLOW
C) BROWN
D) BLACK

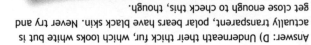

Answer: D) Underneath their thick fur, which looks white but is actually transparent, polar bears have black skin. Never try and get close enough to check this, though.

Polar bears are the biggest land predators on Earth. They can sniff out a seal (or a person) 1.5 kilometres away, even if it's buried under a metre of snow. If you see one, and you have no means of escape (such as a handy helicopter or snowmobile), your only hope is that the bear has already eaten. **If it's hungry, it will eat you.**

! FACTS WIMPS NEED TO KNOW !

POLAR BEAR VITAL STATISTICS

Polar bears are up to 2.5 metres long and weigh up to 720 kilograms (that's probably ten times heavier than your dad).

THE WIMP'S DAD

◦ Polar bears live in the Arctic — in northern Canada, Alaska, Greenland, Russia and Svalbard (a group of Norwegian islands).

◦ They can run at up to 30 km/h (definitely faster than you can).

◦ Despite the fact that a polar bear would happily eat you for breakfast, people aren't usually on the menu, since they're relatively rare in the Arctic. A polar bear's diet consists of seals, mainly, with the odd walrus or washed-up whale carcass.

Bear Necessities

Life is tough for polar bears. They've had to adapt to live in the harsh, freezing conditions of the Arctic, where temperatures can drop to minus 50 degrees Celsius. They have thick fur and 10 centimetres of blubber to keep them warm. Their paws measure 30 centimetres

BELIEVE IT OR NOT...

Although adult polar bears are huge, lumbering great whoppers, at birth, polar bear cubs are only the size of guinea pigs.

across, so that they act like snowshoes, and they have bumps on the bottom to stop them slipping on the ice. But the prey the bears live on is in short supply, and it can usually run or swim faster than a polar bear — in fact, most polar bear hunts aren't successful. No wonder they're cross, and probably hungry and quite likely to eat you. Nom, nom, nom...

FACTS WIMPS NEED TO KNOW

SCARY BEARS

Polar bears are without doubt the most dangerous type of bear, but other kinds of bear have killed and eaten people too. **Here are a few things you should know about scary bears:**

⊘ If you see any kind of bear, keep your distance and move away from it as calmly and quickly as you can (i.e. try not to scream uncontrollably and wave your arms about in panic). Most bears are shy of people, and won't attack unless they think you're threatening their cubs.

⊘ Indian sloth bears live on insects but can be extremely dangerous to humans — one sloth bear killed 12 people before it was caught.

They kill using their massive sword-shaped front claws, which can be 10 centimetres long.

⊙ A grizzly bear's diet is mostly vegetarian, but they sometimes eat animals as big as moose, as well as, um, people.

⊙ Don't try to outrun a grizzly bear — they can belt along at 48 km/h. But if you do need to run away from a grizzly bear, run downhill — grizzlies find it more difficult to run downhill and won't be as fast.

Lions

Lions are
responsible for
hundreds of human deaths in Africa every
year (along with the deaths of quite a lot
of zebra, antelope, etc, obviously). But
they don't generally see humans as part
of their diet. Except sometimes. . .

TERRIFYING TRUE TALES

THE TSAVO LIONS

In 1898 a railway bridge was built
across the Tsavo River in Kenya, in
the territory of two big male lions.
Between March and December, the
lions killed and ate 135 railway workers
(according to reports at the time), many
of whom were dragged from their tents at
night. The lions were eventually shot and
killed. They then spent 25 years as rugs,

before being stuffed and put on display at the Chicago Field Museum. No one is sure why the lions preyed on humans instead of their usual prey, but drought, disease among prey animals, and toothache have all been suggested.

FACTS WIMPS NEED TO KNOW

LION VITAL STATISTICS

⊙ Wild African lions live only in African national parks and game reserves. There's also a small number of Asiatic lions (which look very similar) living in India's Gir forest.

⊙ Male lions measure up to about 2.5 metres long, and weigh up to 250 kilograms.

⊙ Although they sometimes hunt during the day, African lions are mostly nocturnal (which is why they're always lounging about on wildlife documentaries).

● Generally, female lions do the hunting, while the male lions grow impressive-looking manes and fight other male lions.

LIONS ARE THE ONLY BIG CATS TO . . .

A) HUNT CROCODILES
B) EAT VEGETABLES
C) HUNT AS A TEAM
D) EAT ONE ANOTHER

Answer: C). Other big cats hunt alone.

! FACTS WIMPS NEED TO KNOW !

HOW TO AVOID A LION ATTACK

If you're going to visit lion territory, make sure you're in a vehicle (preferably a really big, strong one — consider toughened glass, etc.) and travel with other people, including a knowledgeable guide. And, whatever you do:

◦ **Don't** go walking in lion territory. That would just be asking for trouble.

◦ **Don't** bring your pet dog, which might be viewed as prey by lions (even if you're not).

◦ **Don't** camp within lion territory. Lions are more likely to attack at night, and a fabric tent is unlikely to stop them.

If you do find yourself confronted by a lion, on your own, in the African bush, then . . . oh dear. But you could try these desperate measures:

◦ **Don't** run away. (Running away will be like wiggling a piece of string for a kitten — the lion will run after you.)

◦ **Do** make eye contact — in the hope that the lion will stop seeing you as prey.

◦ **Do** make a noise and wave your arms above your head to make yourself appear bigger. If things go badly, try punching and kicking, aiming at the eyes and head . . . unfortunately, that's also the bit with the teeth.

TERRIFYING TRUE TALES

In 2007, herdsman Moses Lekalau was walking home with his cattle in Maralal, Kenya, when he was attacked by a lion.

Using every ounce of his strength and courage, he managed to kill the lion, using his bare hands and a spear.

Exhausted and wounded, he staggered off towards home . . . only to be set upon by a pack of hyenas!

This was turning into a very bad day for Moses. He fought the vicious wild dogs with what was left of his strength.

A passing motorist stopped and helped to scare the hyenas away, then took Moses to hospital. Sadly, Moses had lost so much blood that he died.

Tigers

Tigers are the biggest of the big cats: they can weigh over 300 kilograms. They're responsible for more human deaths than any other big cat — thousands of people have been killed in India by the Bengal tigers that live there.

Tigers don't usually see people as prey, but some do become "man-eaters". This is often because they're injured and can't catch their usual prey, which is much better at running away than even the most terrified wimp.

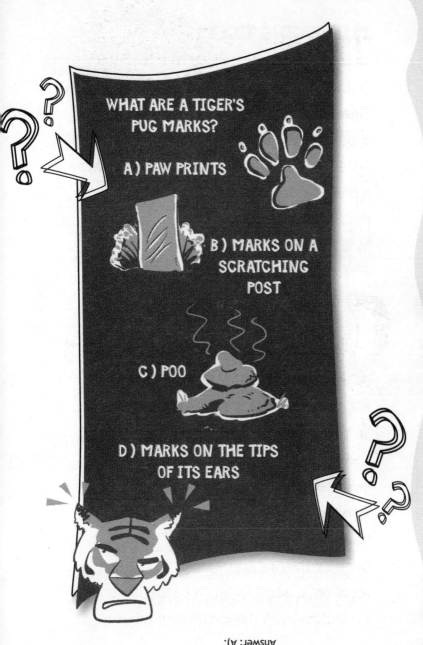

WHAT ARE A TIGER'S PUG MARKS?

A) PAW PRINTS

B) MARKS ON A SCRATCHING POST

C) POO

D) MARKS ON THE TIPS OF ITS EARS

Answer: A).

MAN-EATING TIGERS

In India, people live close to tiger habitats and human deaths occur every year. Some tigers have become famous man-eaters:

Oi! Wake up!

⊙ The **Champawat Tigress** killed 436 people before she was killed in the early 20th century. The tigress had some broken teeth, which would have made it difficult for her to kill deer and other prey animals.

⊙ The **Tigers of Chowgarh** were a pair of tigers that killed at least 64 people between 1925 and 1930 in northern India.

Tigers have the biggest canine teeth of all big cats. This is a human one (left) for size comparison. **Ouch!**

◦ In the Sundarbans, a coastal area on the borders of India and Bangladesh, healthy tigers do prey on people as well as other animals. Tigers are good swimmers and sometimes they attack people fishing from their boats in the mangrove swamps.

The people of the Sundarbans are some of the world's least wimpy: as well as tigers, they have to put up with saltwater crocodiles (see page 64) and sharks (see page 52).

BELIEVE IT OR NOT...

The hard-nut people of the Sundarbans sometimes wear masks on the back of their heads, because tigers usually attack from behind. This worked well for a while – the tigers were fooled and left the people with masks alone. But the tigers are clever and they're learning to identify the face masks.

Despite being the beefiest big cats of the lot, tigers don't have the loudest roar — lions do.

SAD TIGER FACTS

◦ Over the last 100 or so years, tigers have been hunted so much that they're now an endangered species. There used to be hundreds of thousands — now, there might only be around three thousand.

◦ Three types of tiger became extinct in the 20th century — the Bali, Caspian and Javan.

◦ Tigers are still hunted. Their bodies are used in traditional Chinese medicine, or as trophies.

MORE SCARY BIG CATS

* FETCH

⊘ You would be unwise to run away from a cheetah: they're the world's fastest land animals and can sprint at more than 110 km/h. The ancient Egyptians kept them as pets and used them for hunting. (Don't try this at home!)

⊘ Cougars, or mountain lions, live in North and South America. They rarely attack humans, but attacks can be fatal

— three people have been killed by cougars in North America since 2000.

◎ Jaguars live in Central and South America. They're smaller than lions and tigers, but  their jaws have the strongest bite of any big cat: they kill their prey by biting through the skull, and they're capable of biting through a turtle's shell.

◎ Leopards are spotted like jaguars but live in Africa and Asia. They're smaller than jaguars, but more likely to kill people because they live closer to them.

In 2012, a leopard attacked several people in the city of Guwahati in Assam, India, and killed one of them.

Snakes

So, you're thinking, we've heard about things that pounce and maul, but what about things that slither and inject their victims with deadly venom?

MOST TOXIC

The most venomous snake in the world is the inland taipan, or fierce snake, which lives in central Australia. (Some sea snakes' venom is more powerful, but not much of it is delivered in a single bite.) But — good news for wimps — the inland taipan isn't aggressive, it doesn't often come into contact with people, and in fact there are no recorded human deaths from its bite. **Hurray!**

WHICH COUNTRY IS HOME
TO MOST OF THE
WORLD'S TOP TEN
VENOMOUS SNAKES?
A) THAILAND
B) AUSTRALIA
C) SOUTH AFRICA
D) INDIA

Answer: B). It's Australia, good thing it's round the other side of the world, that is, unless you actually live there. . .

FACTS WIMPS NEED TO KNOW

INLAND TAIPAN

◊ Many deadly animals are brightly coloured as a warning, but the inland taipan is brown or olive green, giving it good camouflage. Keep a keen eye out!

◊ Inland taipans grow up to 2.5 metres long.

◊ They live on the hot, dry grasslands of central Australia and live on rodents . . .

◊ . . . yet there's enough venom in an inland taipan's bite to kill a hundred people! *Gaaaa!*

GOOD NEWS FOR WIMPS

If you live in the UK, the adder is the only
venomous snake that could bother you.
(And it probably won't.) Since 1876,
there have only been 14 reported
deaths due to its bite.

Did you say that adders are venomous?

MOST DEADLY

On the other hand . . . in India, there are more than ten thousand human deaths from snake bites every year. The main culprits are the **Indian cobra** and **Russell's viper**.

The **carpet viper** kills hundreds of people in Africa every year, and so does the **Egyptian cobra** and the **puff adder**.

Watch out for flying snakes! They can glide from tree branches for up to 100 metres. Luckily, they're not dangerous to people.

WHICH TYPE OF ANIMAL
IS THE WORLD'S
MOST POISONOUS?
A) SNAKE
B) SCORPION
C) FROG
D) JELLYFISH

Answer: C). The golden poison dart frog, which lives in Colombia, is the world's most poisonous creature. The tiny frogs are only 5 centimetres long but have enough poison on their skin to kill ten adult humans. By the way, there's a difference between poisonous — you will be poisoned if you eat or (in some cases) touch the creature — and venomous — where the poison is injected into your body via an animal's fangs or sting.

!FACTS WIMPS NEED TO KNOW!!

HOW TO AVOID A SNAKE BITE

⊘ Don't wear flip-flops or similar flimsy footwear in areas where there might be snakes. That's asking for trouble!

⊘ It's unlikely that you'd ever be tempted, but **never** try to handle a snake — not even a dead one. Amazingly, a dead snake can still bite!

⊘ If you discover a snake in a confined space, do not corner it — some snakes will strike if they can't see an escape route.

◦ Some snakes, such as the African black mamba, can be aggressive if you stray into their territory. So if you see a snake and it's looking cross, back away slowly.

◦ Some good advice in any circumstances: don't stick your hands into dark crevices — who knows what might be lurking in there?

IF YOU ARE BITTEN BY A SNAKE:

◦ Get to hospital! Fast!

◦ Don't wash the wound — medical staff will take a swab to find out what type of snake bit you.

◦ Don't apply a tourniquet, cut the wound, try to suck out the poison, or any of the other daft things they do in movies when someone's bitten by a snake. You'll probably only make it worse.

CONSTRICTORS

Constricting snakes, such as pythons, don't
have venom. They kill their prey by squeezing.
Every time the prey animal breathes out, the
snake squeezes more tightly, until finally
the prey animal can't breathe at all.
Reticulated pythons are the longest snakes
in the world — the longest recorded was
9.74 metres long — and they could easily
squeeze a person to death. The good news
is that they don't. At least,
not very often.

Anyway, you
probably

Hmmnh!

CUDDLES

shouldn't worry about being killed by a
constricting snake, unless you keep one as
a pet (which, especially for wimps, is a
very bad idea).

BELIEVE IT OR NOT...

Reticulated pythons can eat prey
as big as deer and wild boar whole.
They open their specially hinged
jaws so that they separate
completely. It doesn't look very
pretty. The snakes have to keep
warm to digest the food before
it rots. Sometimes a python's
afternoon nap – after a really
big lunch – can last months.

Hippopotamuses

Hippos? Those fat, jolly vegetarians that loll about happily singing **Mud, Mud, Glorious Mud?** It's a shame to disillusion you but, far from their popular cuddly image, hippos are in fact extremely dangerous beasts. They are responsible for more deaths per year than any other African wild animal. Step away from the swamp. . .

Wimp Rating: 8.5 out of 10

HUNGRY HIPPOS

Hippos are huge. They can be 3.5 metres long, 1.5 metres tall, and weigh 3.2 tonnes. (There are trucks that weigh less than that.) Hippos are vegetarian, but they are very territorial

and aggressive, and they have enormous teeth. Their mouths can open more than a metre wide, and their tusk-like teeth can be 70 centimetres long.

FACTS WIMPS NEED TO KNOW

If you're canoeing in Botswana in Africa
and you spot a hippo, the chances are it will
leave you alone . . . but you can't be sure.
Your chances of survival could hinge on the
following information:

◎ Don't keep going towards it! **Stop!**
Go back! Quick! (But keep calm.)

◎ Don't get in the way of a hippo's route
to water or its young. This will make it
very cross.

○ Don't try to get a closer view of the hippo's cute baby. There is nothing — **nothing** — that will enrage a hippo more.

○ Don't assume that the hippo is opening its cavernous mouth to yawn — it is threatening you, you fool! Retreat!

Yawn!

BELIEVE IT OR NOT. . .
Hippos have been known to bite crocodiles in half – usually when the crocs get too close to a baby hippo.

UNDERWATER KILLERS

Sooooo . . . you thought you'd hide in the water, huh? Well, hello! There are also killer animals in the oceans and seas.

Now it's time to swim, not run!

Sharks

A WIMP'S WORST NIGHTMARE

You're on holiday, swimming off the coast of Florida. People start waving to you from the beach. You give a cheery wave back, and swim a bit further out. Suddenly, something grazes painfully against your leg and it starts to bleed — you turn to see a horrifying sight: a huge triangular fin slicing through the water towards you. . .

Aaarrgggh! It's a huge shark! And it's coming for you with its hideous, gaping mouth wide open, revealing hundreds of huge serrated teeth!

THE WIMP's HAPPY PLACE

Gaaaa! You might want to lie on the sofa for a bit and go to your "happy place". Wimps the world over get panic-stricken at the thought of being eaten by an enormous fish . . . which isn't all that surprising. But sharks probably aren't as dangerous as you might think.

GOOD NEWS FOR WIMPS

There are about 350 different types of shark, but less than 10 per cent of them have been known to attack humans, and only three kinds regularly attack them. "Regularly" sounds pretty bad, but in fact there are only about 70 shark attacks on people every year around the world, and fewer than ten end in death.

Shoes, antlers, licence plates and part of a suit of armour have all been found inside tiger sharks' stomachs.

Millions of people swim in the sea every year, so that makes your chances of being eaten alive by a giant fish very small indeed. There are plenty of other sea creatures that are far more dangerous than sharks. There, that's made you feel better now, hasn't it?

WHERE DO MOST SHARK
ATTACKS HAPPEN?
A) SOUTH AFRICA
B) UNITED STATES
C) AUSTRALIA
D) MALAYSIA

Answer: B). On average, most shark attacks happen on the east coast of the United States.

GREAT WHITES, TIGERS AND BULLS

If you find yourself in the sea surrounded by fins, snapping jaws and red foam, one of these types of shark is likely to be the culprit:

Yeeeuw!

○ **Great white sharks** are absolutely massive — up to 7 metres long — and live in warmer seas. They usually prey on seals, and they're quite fussy eaters. So, if a great white mistakes you for a seal and takes a bite, it will probably spit it out and swim off. That's the good news. Now for the not-so-good news. An adult great white is BIG, so you could be dead before it discovers you're not that tasty. Told you it was not-so-good news.

◦ **Tiger sharks** measure up to 3.5 metres long. They like warmer seas too, but are more likely to stay close to the coast. They're not at all fussy, and will eat car tyres and any other junk they find. So, even though people aren't their usual prey, if they take a bite out of you they won't care how you taste.

◦ **Bull sharks** are aggressive and tend to live in shallower coastal waters — where people like to swim. They grow up to about 2.5 metres long and can live in fresh water as well as sea water, so they've been known to swim up rivers and surprise people. **Boo!**

TERRIFYING TRUE TALES

If you're attacked by a shark, the chances are you'll survive — even though sharks have up to 300 teeth! One survivor had a bit of help. . . Todd Endris was sitting on his surfboard off the Californian coast in 2007, when a 5-metre-long great white shark attacked. The shark ripped the skin off his back and bit Todd's leg, while Todd kicked it in the snout with his other leg.

Then — and this really did happen, honestly — a pod of bottlenose dolphins arrived and formed a ring around Todd, so that he was able to make it back to the beach. He had lost a lot of blood but he survived, scarred but otherwise fine.

Dolphins and porpoises are our friends. In 2010, Actor Dick Van Dyke said he was rescued by a pod of porpoises when he drifted out to sea on his surfboard.

Box Jellyfish

On a beautiful sandy beach in northern Queensland, Australia, the waves glitter invitingly in the sun. But, whatever you do, **DON'T GO INTO THE SEA!** Don't even paddle! Because, beneath the surface of those glittering waves, deadly assassins await. . .

Even though box jellyfish don't see you as prey and can't move very fast, they are incredibly dangerous because of their fast-acting, lethal venom.

WARNING! DO NOT SWIM HERE, OR THIS WILL HAPPEN TO YOU.

(An example of a warning sign on a beach.)

⊙ They are also called stingers, are found in northern Australia, the west Indo-Pacific, and Southeast Asia.

BOX JELLYFISH VITAL STATISTICS

⊙ There are two types of box jellyfish that are dangerous to humans. The most deadly is about 25 centimetres in diameter and has around 60 stinging tentacles, which are up to 3 metres long.

⊙ Their venom is one of the world's most powerful natural poisons. It can kill a human being in three minutes.

◎ The poison is delivered via the box jellyfish's stinging tentacles. It's so painful that people sometimes go into shock and drown, or die of heart failure, before the venom kills them.

◎ Box jellyfish developed their super-powerful venom to kill fast-moving prey (fish and prawns) immediately, so that it doesn't get away or damage the jellyfish's delicate tentacles as it struggles.

◎ If you are desperate to swim in an area where you might be fatally stung and die an agonising death, wear a "stinger suit" to stop the tentacles coming into contact with your skin.

◎ To make life even more difficult, box jellyfish are virtually transparent, so they're almost impossible to spot.

Crocodiles

If the thought of lethal stinging tentacles makes you shudder, how about being snapped in the jaws of the world's biggest crocodile and eaten alive?

Wimp Rating: 9 out of 10

The biggest crocodile on Earth is the saltwater crocodile. They're also known as "salties", which makes them sound friendly — but they're not. In fact, saltwater crocodiles are the animals most likely to eat people.

Whereas other underwater predators won't see you as prey, a saltwater crocodile most certainly will. The same is true of Nile crocodiles, by the way, so don't go near one of those either.

BELIEVE IT OR NOT. . .
Even sedated salties aren't safe! In 2007, a vet at a zoo in Taiwan had his arm bitten off by a sedated saltwater crocodile. The arm was retrieved and reattached.

FACTS WIMPS NEED TO KNOW

SALTWATER CROCODILE VITAL STATISTICS

๏ Salties live in eastern India, northern Australia, and Southeast Asia. They can live in salt water and fresh water.

๏ They can be up to 7 metres long — as wide as a football goalmouth — and weigh 450 kilograms.

◎ A saltie's bite is stronger than that of any other animal.

◎ Salties often lie in wait by the water's edge. When something, or someone, comes close enough, they launch themselves from the water, grab the prey and dive down to drown it, before tearing it apart.

◎ They prey on fish as well as much larger animals, such as cattle, wild boar . . . and people. One crocodile even ate a Bengal tiger.

TERRIFYING TRUE TALE

SALTIE ATTACK

If a large saltwater crocodile attacks you, the chances are you won't have time to think about how to defend yourself before you're dragged underwater, drowned and feasted upon. But occasionally people do escape. . .

Todd Bairstow was attacked by a 3-metre-long saltwater crocodile while he was fishing in a creek in northern Queensland, Australia, in 2011. The creature bit off one of his fingers and broke both his legs as it tried to drag him

BANG BANG
BANG THUMP
THUMP BANG

into the water. Todd held on to the roots of a mangrove and bashed, kicked and gouged the crocodile's eyes for half an hour, until finally someone heard his screams and came to help, beating the crocodile with a stick until it finally gave up.

HOW TO AVOID THE JAWS OF A SALTWATER CROCODILE

◊ Don't go anywhere near water in saltwater crocodile territory.

◊ If you see a saltwater crocodile, climb a tree — you won't be able to outrun it or outswim it, but at least crocodiles can't climb trees.

◊ Er. . .

◊ That's it.

TINY ASSASSINS

71

Mosquitos

Wimp Rating:
8.5 out of 10

Mosquitos are probably the
most dangerous insects on the planet because
they spread the deadly disease malaria.

FACTS WIMPS NEED TO KNOW

MOSQUITO VITAL STATISTICS

⊘ Malaria isn't carried by all mosquitos,

just the female
anopheles
mosquito. They're
found in Africa,
the Middle East,
South America and
parts of Europe.

◊ Malaria is caused by a parasite, which gets injected into a person's bloodstream via the mosquito's bite.

◊ If you're travelling to a country that has a risk of malaria, take anti-malaria tablets, sleep under a mosquito net, use lots of insect repellent and cover up your skin.

◊ Over a million people die from malaria every year, although the disease isn't usually fatal if it's treated early enough.

◊ Mosquitos like to bite some people more than others depending on blood type (they prefer blood type O).

MORE FATAL FLIES

A horsefly bite is painful but at least it can't kill you. Tsetse flies are quite similar to horseflies (they're yellow or brown and about 1.5 centimetres long), and their bite feels the

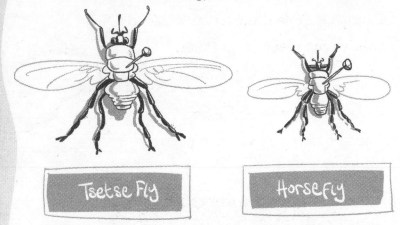

Tsetse Fly

Horsefly

same, but unfortunately they can kill you. While they suck your blood they can also give you a nasty parasite that causes a horrible and often fatal disease known as sleeping sickness. Tsetse flies that carry the disease are found in 36 African countries. Sometimes victims don't know they have sleeping sickness for weeks or even months, by which time it's very difficult to treat.

In South America, Chagas' disease, caused by the same type of parasite, is spread by (look away now if you're squeamish) the poo of insects called kissing bugs. Chagas' disease can kill you too. Both diseases cause tens of thousands of deaths every year. Keep a fly swat within reach at all times.

FLIES ARE ALSO RESPONSIBLE FOR CARRYING WHICH OF THESE DISEASES?

A) DYSENTERY, CHOLERA AND TYPHOID FEVER.

B) MEASLES, MUMPS AND CHICKENPOX.

C) SCARLET FEVER, ASTHMA AND COLITIS.

D) BUBONIC PLAGUE, GOUT AND PNEUMONIA.

Answer: A). All three diseases can be fatal.

Spiders

Wimp Rating:
6 out of 10

Millions of people are
frightened of spiders. After all, they scuttle
alarmingly fast, they have far too many legs
and eyes, and they're just plain creepy. But
most spiders are completely harmless, and
they're absolutely titchy. For goodness' sake
– **pull yourself together!**

BIG HAIRY SPIDERS

Actually, not all spiders are titchy.
The biggest spider in the world is
the Goliath bird-eating spider.

It's the size of a dinner plate, and it's hairy
and mean-looking, with fangs 2.5 centimetres
long. But you don't really have anything to
fear from the Goliath — a type of tarantula.
It preys on mice and other small creatures,
and even if it does bite you its venom
wouldn't hurt much. In fact, there are no
reported deaths from the bite of any tarantula
spider. By the way, there's a spider with an
even larger leg-span — giant huntsman spiders
measure 30 centimetres across!

VENOMOUS SPIDERS

There are some spiders
whose bite can be fatal
to humans, though.
Most aren't aggressive towards
people, but they do tend to live close
to people in towns, where they lurk
in dark places. The animals most
in danger from spider bites are
insects and other small
creatures — but there
are some spiders
you'll want to
keep clear of.

BRAZILIAN WANDERING SPIDERS

These spiders live in South America (they were first discovered in Brazil) but can turn up inside bunches of bananas all over the world. You might never look at a bunch of bananas in quite the same way again. . .

They are big (up to 10 centimetres!), hairy, aggressive . . . and they can jump. They are probably the most venomous spiders in the world. Their venom can kill within minutes. They scuttle into dark places during the day, then come out to do their wandering at night.

TERRIFYING TRUE TALE

In 2005, a Brazilian wandering spider stowed away in a crate of bananas and was found lurking under a dishcloth in a Somerset pub kitchen by the chef, Matthew Stevens. Unfortunately, he only discovered the spider was there when he picked up the dishcloth and it bit him. The spider bit him again when he tried to catch it. Luckily, Matthew took a photo of the creature with his phone. He was

Oh, Mummy!

taken to hospital with a very swollen hand and difficulty breathing, and quickly got worse. Medical staff sent the photo to Bristol Zoo, who identified the spider. Matthew was given the antivenom. Without the photo, he might have died.

HOW MANY EYES
DOES A SPIDER HAVE?
A) TWO
B) FOUR
C) SIX
D) EIGHT

Answer: All the answers are right. Most spiders have eight eyes, though there are some (including recluse spiders) that have six, and there are also spiders that have four, two, or even no eyes. Despite most spiders' many eyes, they can't see very well, apart from wolf spiders and jumping spiders, which have big, prominent eyes. Urrghh.

SOME OTHER SPIDERS TO AVOID

⊘ Black widow spiders are small (4 centimetres wide), but they have powerful venom that can kill people. They're found in North America and also in Sweden, where they were probably imported from the USA in new cars. Redback spiders are relatives of black widows, and are found in Australia. Hundreds of people end up in hospital every year from redback and black widow bites.

⊘ Sydney funnel-web spiders are some of the most feared spiders in Australia. They're up to about 5 centimetres across, and their bite is venomous. Horrifyingly, the spider's fangs are supposed to be capable of biting through a human fingernail. **Gah!**

⊙ Brown recluse spiders are small (2 centimetres wide) and found in the south and central USA. Their venom can cause human tissue to die, creating a very nasty wound.

BELIEVE IT OR NOT...

In 2002, a home in Kansas, USA, was infested with brown recluse spiders. A shudder-inducing 2,055 of them were collected — and yet no one living in the house was bitten.

Scorpions

A WIMP'S WORST NIGHTMARE

You're on holiday in Egypt. You get out of bed
one morning and shuffle into your slippers
and. . .

Yeeooow!

You scream as a searing pain shoots into your
toe and throughout your foot and lower leg.
It feels as though you've been shot with an
arrow! Out of one of your slippers scuttles a
small, yellow scorpion. **A death stalker!**

DEATH STALKER SCORPIONS

Death stalker scorpions are the world's most venomous scorpions, but, despite that and the scary sounding name, only 3 per cent of people who are stung by them have a severe reaction. So — good news! You're very unlikely to have a bad reaction to a scorpion's sting, but if you do, these are the symptoms:

- Numbness all over your body
- Blurred vision
- Difficulty swallowing and breathing
- Oh, and quite possibly, death.

Still, let's stick to the bright side. As long as you can get to hospital you'll be all right, because there is an antivenom.

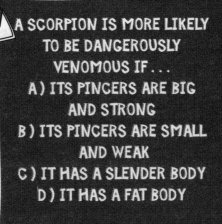

A SCORPION IS MORE LIKELY TO BE DANGEROUSLY VENOMOUS IF . . .
A) ITS PINCERS ARE BIG AND STRONG
B) ITS PINCERS ARE SMALL AND WEAK
C) IT HAS A SLENDER BODY
D) IT HAS A FAT BODY

Answer: B). The size of a scorpion's pincers is a good way of measuring how powerful its venom might be. If the pincers are small and weak, it will need venom to paralyse its prey because the pincers probably won't be strong enough to stop it escaping.

BELIEVE IT OR NOT. . .

Kanchana Ketkaew, from Thailand, is known as the Scorpion Queen. She lived in a glass box full of scorpions for 33 days. The box measured 12 square metres and contained 5,320 scorpions. The Scorpion Queen was stung 13 times. She's married to the Centipede King, who spent 28 days in a box with 1,000 centipedes.

I think I just sat on one.

Last Word

You've been very brave. You've come face to face with big, hairy spiders, crocodile-chomping hippos and venomous snakes, and you've encountered animals that can sting, maul or squeeze you to death. Now, you're armed with vital information on how to keep as far away from them as possible.

But you might have noticed something from this book: unless you're determined to swim in seas full of lethal jellyfish or go for a stroll in lion country, you're really very unlikely to meet a horrible death in the jaws of a killer animal.

There are plenty of far more scary things for a wimp to worry about. . .

Your Wimp Rating

Answer these questions with "yes" or "no". How many do you answer "yes" to? Add up the number to generate your very own wimp rating on page 91 — go on, how tough are you really?

Wimp Rating: ?? out of 10

1. A friend is taking a "Swim The River" challenge in hippo territory, and asks you to join them. You say. . .

2. The Scorpion Queen invites you into her glass box. You say. . .

3. You're offered the chance to go shark diving. You say. . .

4. You're in Queensland, Australia. A friend says, "Let's go surfing, the water looks lovely and sparkly." You say. . .

5. Someone asks you if you'll help to get the saltie out of their swimming pool. You say. . .

6. Mosquitos are just flying bugs; they can't hurt you. Do you agree?

7. You're fishing in the Sundarbans, you're wearing your mask, but you're feeling really hot. Do you take off your mask to cool down?

8. A friend decides to wear her new flip-flops on a snake trail safari. Do you copy her?

9. A friend asks for help to find their pet snake, which has gone missing. You say. . .

10. You'd be happy to have a Brazilian wanderer run across your hand.

How many questions did you answer "yes" to?

Three questions: you're a novice wimp – you're on the path to great wimpness.

Four questions: you're a wannabe wimp — keep trying.

Five questions: you're as tough as old boots (with a scorpion in).

Six questions: you've got a bite like a shark.

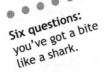

Seven questions: you're super-inland-taipan-snake scary.

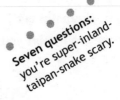

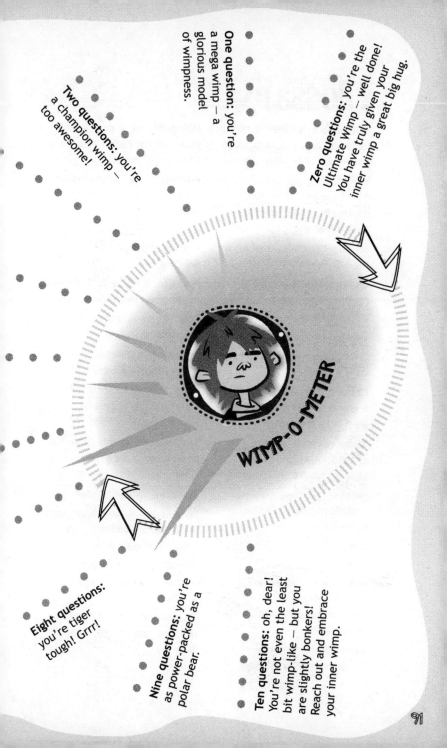

Zero questions: you're the Ultimate Wimp — well done! You have truly given your inner wimp a great big hug.

One question: you're a mega wimp — a glorious model of wimpness.

Two questions: you're a champion wimp — too awesome!

WIMP-O-METER

Eight questions: you're tiger tough! Grrr!

Nine questions: you're power-packed as a polar bear.

Ten questions: oh, dear! You're not even the least bit wimp-like — but you are slightly bonkers! Reach out and embrace your inner wimp.

Glossary

Antivenom a medical product that is used to treat poisonous bites from snakes or insects

Blood type human blood divides into four main types: A, B, AB and O

Blubber thick layer of body fat

Camouflage markings or skin colour that make an animal difficult to spot

Carcass a dead body

Cavernous similar to a huge cave in size

Extinct a type of animal, or a group of animals, that have died out completely

Game reserve a large area of land set aside for wild animals to live there safely

Habitat the place where certain plants and animals like to live

Malaria a fever spread by mosquitos

Mangrove swamps areas where mangroves, which are trees and shrubs that can live in salt water, live

Maul injure something through rough treatment

Mosquito net a fine net, especially around a bed, to keep away insects

National park an important area of countryside that is protected

Nocturnal active at night: moving about, eating and hunting

Parasite a lifeform that lives off another lifeform

Pod the name for a group of dolphins or whales

Predator an animal that hunts other animals

Prey to hunt animals for food/animals that other animals hunt for food

Sedated when an animal has been given a drug to make it sleepy and calm

Serrated a jagged edge

Snowshoes wide frames that are attached to boots, to help them walk on snow

Territory the area of land that the animal considers to be theirs

Tourniquet a tight bandage or cloth used to stop blood flow

Websites

http://www.polarbearsinternational.org/polar-bears/ bear-essentials-polar-style This website features tons of polar bear facts, along with interactive Arctic maps — so you don't have to go there yourself.

http://video.nationalgeographic.com/video/ animals/reptiles-animals/snakes On this website there's a whole range of very cool snake videos to watch from the safety of your sofa.

http://www.bbc.co.uk/nature/ life/Spider Lots of facts, photos and awesome videos of other people picking up dangerous spiders.

http://animal.discovery.com/tv-shows/animal-planet-presents/videos/maneaters-saltwater-crocodiles.htm Stay out of harm's way with these crocodile videos (contains advertising).

Index

Africa 20, 22, 25, 35, 40, 43, 46, 48, 72, 74
Arctic 15, 16
Australia 36, 37, 38, 55, 60, 61, 66, 68, 82
Bangladesh 31
bears 7, 11, 12—19
    grizzly bears 19
    Indian sloth bears 18, 19
    polar bears 11, 12—18
box jellyfish 41, 60—63, 88

Chagas' disease 75
cheetahs 34
cougars 34, 35
crocodiles 23, 31, 49, 64—69, 88

dolphins 59

Endris, Todd 58—59

fish 8, 52-59, 63, 67
frogs, golden poison dart 41

hippopotamuses 46—49, 88
horseflies 74

India 22, 28, 30—31, 35, 37, 40, 66

jaguars 35

Kenya 20—21, 26—27
Ketkaew, Kanchana 87
kissing bugs 75

leopards 35
lions 20—27, 33, 35, 88
    Tsavo lions 20—21

malaria 72—72
mosquitos 8, 72—73

polar bears 11, 12—18

scorpions 6, 41, 84—87
    death stalker scorpions 84, 85
sharks 31, 52—59
    bull sharks 57
    great white sharks 56, 58, 59
    tiger sharks 54, 57
sleeping sickness 74
snakes 7, 36—45, 88
    adders 39, 40
    black mambas 43
    cobras 40
    inland taipans 36, 37, 38
    pythons 44—45
    Russell's vipers 40
South America 34, 35, 72, 75, 79
spiders 76—83, 88
    black widow spiders 82
    Brazilian wandering spiders 79—81
    brown recluse spiders 81, 83
    Goliath bird-eating spiders 77
    huntsman spiders 77
    redback spiders 82
    Sydney funnel-web spiders 82, 83
Sundarbans, the 31, 32

tigers 6, 28—33, 35, 67
    Champawat Tigress 30
    Tigers of Chowgarh 30
tsetse flies 74

United States 52, 53, 55, 58, 59, 82, 83

The WiMP'S GUIDE TO

illustrated by
Dave Smith

JUNGLE SURVIVAL

by
Tracey Turner

978 1 4451 1461 3 pb   978 1 4451 1465 1 eBook

Have you ever:

Paddled down the Amazon River? ✗
Been stung by a scorpion? ✗
Gone without food for a day? ✗

If you answered NO to all of the above then this is the book for you!

Terrified of bugs? Great! Feel sick about
travelling? Fantastic! Inside you can read
about loads of crazy stuff and how
to survive – or avoid it.

Love your inner wimp!

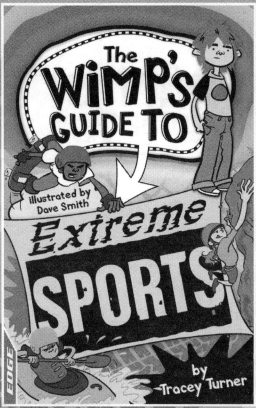

The Wimp's Guide to Extreme SPORTS

illustrated by Dave Smith

by Tracey Turner

978 1 4451 1460 6 pb   978 1 4451 1464 4 eBook

Have you ever:

Climbed Mount Everest? ✗
Been a skateboarding champion? ✗
Won a race at school sports day? ✗

**If you answered NO to all of the above
then this is the book for you!**

Scared of heights? Great! Feel green
about extreme sports? Super! Inside you
can read about loads of crazy stuff
and how to survive – or avoid it.

Love your inner wimp!